almond, eyeless

almond, eyeless

Karen Meadows

groundhog
POETRY PRESS

2018

Library of Congress Control Number: 2018934016

ISBN: 978-0-9976766-8-6

Printed in the United States

Published by

Groundhog Poetry Press LLC

6915 Ardmore Drive

Roanoke, Virginia 24019-4403

www.groundhogpoetrypress.com

The groundhog logo is the registered trademark ™ of Groundhog
Poetry Press LLC.

For Tim

CONTENTS

The Idea

that we can neighbor,
side by side, like two
red Bantam cocks,
persona a persona.

Purchase

The notebook-cover–blue print
on my serrated-end receipt
for your debut collection
states I paid sixty cents tax,
pushing the cost over twelve
dollars to unearth your saviors
and their methods of marching
flat out onto the page like ants
en route in Lagrangian Ls.

These saints attempt an excuse
for me to replant from dorm
hallway to bookcased office,
because their mannered pulse points
slanty-match the tried voice in my iambs,
which amount to the clean thought:
similarity is a basis for relationship.

I synchronize foot placement
to the default setting of each
rise and run, steep and mirrored

by the next, until a knock

shoots over the swirled wood

of your office door, vacant

as unleft voicemail, winding

my stride counterclockwise to let

it rattle home repeating:

life is not mathematical.

En Garde

Nothin's shakin' in this tangled firework
of goldrushing half-flag semaphores stretched
out like pews in the hissy fits of strobes
that signal the melt of the overtuned,
inked pupils of attaboys,

so I nudge the turnstile
of a secondhand hour that sweet-talks
the shake of our ho-hum smiles,
unaware we both know
Beethoven was short.

Crocodile Man to Monkey Woman

My hands become scalar,
laddered texture,
to summon your stunted grace,
sawed-off and eclectic,
into the dirt with me.

I lean you
into the adeptness of wandering,
ungluing you
from the ones who can commit,
who raised you to believe
that women with beards are sideshows
(and they are).

          Against the backdrop
of secondary tents and line-ups of deformity,
you do swing untethered from a shaven youth
despite a constant sifting through
what is weak

(instant coffee, diet tea, me)

and tailored by your first job offer

as a feature attraction,

roadside product placement,

marketed strictly on the premise

that any story is funny

with a monkey in it.

for Mack Reed

Kate at Rader

"Don't die wondering" —an eighth-
-grade-Kevin-Roberts reference
you quoted in the slack clothesline curve
of our last conversation before boarding
the suppository-shaped jet to California
            (a blank state
worth a dart throw even though
the coast chats honeymoon or anniversary
vacation, not a long-shot antidote
or Bergeron process to snow emotions
            like an IV drip
of spinal instructions that toss the luteous
polluted quarter moon that paces
your eyes for your body, point A
to point B, a mile of returns along
the Rothko strip of red tiled
from bed to cafeteria, where the faces,
            halogen-pale
lollipop heads, birth an air
of Hollywood like the trim palm
fronds that rub in the sounds

of shuffling crinoline and the cold

reiteration of the Pacific as a Rader

greeter held a name sign

    half-mast

with the svelte print of *Kathleen*

at baggage claim, each line in each

letter a piling of ticks on the scale,

    a system

of ounces that made you question

the payoff for standing heavier,

and if Kevin Roberts meant by what he said:

    not dying

in wonder is playing to win—a scratch

at the Big Lotto squares to uncover

in silver filings two thick matching slatted

    palm trunks).

Charged with Error

I lived with a starving snake.
It was not my snake.
My room had the space
for the 30-gallon tank,
which was suddenly there
when I came home for break.
His name was Job, a ball python.
Yes, he eventually died.

I think back for signs,
but snakes don't mew or whine,
or butt their heads against glass.
Snakes do not show desperation.
They barely move;
pet snakes, anyway,
starving or not.

As far as I knew, he was being fed.
Once, I watched.
A live white rat,
nose fidgeting but not scared.

The snake showed a slight clench

of muscle, like a woman sucking in

her stomach for a photo.

Yes, a shutter snap, just like that:

scales like honeycomb cloisonné

knotted around white pelt.

The air escaped, with breaks,

as the rat was compacted

like a car; the crush of bones

was quiet clicks, the crack

of knuckles. No blood.

Can't snakes live months on one meal?

Perhaps I should have asked.

Honestly, he scared me.

Heat pits lining his mouth

in half smiles: caverns of baby-pink

skin sourcing mine as I slept.

His urine was a white blob on a log—

a press of titanium white paint on palette.

He was a reminder

that I, too, was hedged in by glass,

nosing at the rocks weighting my ceiling screen

with what, to others, seemed plain curiosity.

My best friend was gone. *Going*, I should say.

But it was clear she was starving. I could hear

the curt bass of her stomach's growls,

see her skin tucked up like an eyelid

in the eave of each rib,

feel her withdrawal as one might a splinter.

Back for summer, the tank was gone.

I wanted to ask, but I knew.

I let a snake die.

It was 20 years ago.

It wasn't my snake.

Bones of Luray

Who knows how it happens
when the decision is made for you —
the red field, flash flooding,
full-body scalping by the rain;
flushed through the cavern's mid-yawn
opening, deposited drowned,
to root at the base of a cave.

The darkness lengthens. Tin-clinks
of water dripping, rowing out
ripples in the mirror pond —
the only reason to listen while lodged
beneath a palate of stalactite
incisors, collecting a shawl of iron:
the nesting of indifference.

Even if picked off the scene
by some rescuer or entrepreneur
needing to know the meaning of *end*,
still, nothing would be quiet
in an installation of bone behind glass —
fragments of remnants, a landmark of absences.

Home Babies

Captioned with spindles, Mary drapes her gaze
in the stone corner, curio-caught,
screened in like a porch
to shrine the Sisters' good work at Tuam:

a septic tank-cum-tholos for home babies
hilled to a hive of spines, ribs, and knots
of skulls—trophies of ideas unborn—
that fall apart in crumbs.

The caretaker knew, so lent his days
tending, clearing when weeds went fraught,
to say: taking guards what is torn
and skates by, like clouds in their casings, dumb.

Oh, Mary, your mantle is a maze
used for feeling where feeling is naught,
a bird-egg–blue coffer of forced remorse
that forgives fathers who lapse into men,

without consequence, or a stint as slave
in a life made to live unwanted;
where hyperdulia feigns the caretaker's torch
and consigns your downcast glance, though absent a son.

Ebb

Yes is a white lab coat,
a windshield crashed, cleared,
an uncorroborated nod
of the head that is sill
to the apron of snow white sheet
doming over wolds of knees.

Candidacy is in the skin's soil,
a sepulcher dark as a checkmark
or peat that stained the sacrifices
of Celtic kings, bloodlet,
bog-lost for centuries.

The patina of bruises stars and spreads
like blended glazes cured in kilns,
causing a wince if pressed, a clawed
punch of lightning through bones unset.

Pain says yes.

A test of the injection streams

like girls from Atomic City,

adjusting dials, slim and pretty;

filing back to the dorms, forth

to the calutrons exhaling dust

flaked fine as carrot seed.

Fifteen teeth marked for extraction

after fractures falsely threatened infection,

after bone was cored for specimen

from legs limply hitched like a marionette's—

prey for the hawks to pick.

They are in no rush.

Anita

Mouths in easy chairs mouth mock surprise.

Describe it once again for me, please:
the leak from private to pubic to public to polygraph.
Oh, those explosive plosives—/p/, /p/, /p/. Make them go on.
Sure can't stand up now—the scorn!

We know you were thinking it, Howell.
We know you were thinking it.

She chose rows of gold buttons, doubled down over
her breasts. Oops, I said it.
It's not too bad.
So, repeat it: breasts, breasts, breasts.

We know you were thinking it, Arlen.
We know you were thinking it.

Introduce your family seated behind you.
Go on, now. Pull that long mic silver,
cock-poised, closer. Otherwise we can't

hear you. Lean in, lean in.

We know you were thinking it, Joe.
We know you were thinking it.

Again is rarely once, is rarely odd, is rarely enough.
Again is a lynching.

Cross-sectioned on a slide—
Now, go on quiet in your quiet life.

Simultaneity (Drunk Text from Contractor, Instructions at Book Fair)

Are you at a slow burn
or a pleasant roasted
marshmallow, toasted brown?

Stay closed till the play ends.
Work security now;
kids, books, after-school hours—
things disappear.

I had to tell a lifelong friend
her grandson killed himself. I knew
her husband, kids and all her dogs.

It's a 60s theme. Wear tie-dye,
headbands, Birks—anything groovy.
The lava lamps take time to heat up.

Nothing can ever prepare you
for trying to help a friend
from falling to pieces . . .
a bottle of good bourbon,

sleep in the hallway
when the screams start,
know the firearms have been hidden.

More stock arrived today.
The diaries sell well.
Refill the erasers.
Empty boxes go under the table.

Life can be truly cruel.
Only close friends can be helpful —
knowing they will listen to me
crying in the corner —
the handshake and a hug
of one more visitor to the darkness.

All sales are taxable.
You can give change on checks.
Memorize the steps for returns.

Thank you for listening.
I value your understanding.

Thank you! None of this
would be possible without volunteers.

Hadley

abstraction is
violation

simplification is
exhaustion

creation is
isolation

gestation is
compensation

station is
destruction

absolution is
illusion

completion is
justification

dedication was
concession

Slug on Strawberry

In another June
the fireflies silently sigh their confessions—
silent as a pulse of heat lightning,
silent as slugs on strawberries
mowing wound-canals,
spatchcocking the fruits through
to their foreheads, white as a Beluga whale's.

Spiders hie, with their own nascent white
hanging from their hulls, over the streams
of mylar shimmer and the stolons that reach
away to thrust up tussocks of pinked triptych canopies
to reconstruct streets of unripe lanterns
flecked with sanded stars, until the season
subsides, osmotically, like guilt.

The Thaw

How nice to have the self left out awhile
like a Catherine Chalmers roach anesthetized
from fifteen minutes in the fridge,
lifted from a clear-pink plastic terrarium
to be painted and positioned:

stem-green with satin-finished red florets
in a dirtbox of Kalanchoe.
The buds, rubber-nosed, loom like colossal heads
until the panic of waking in single strobe-cracks
of flood lightning to realize one is scenery
on a staircase of stalks,
an imposter beetle at best.

They nosedive, antennae tuned, testing the air
for angels who might self-scoop out of the fake
background sky to collect them:
the lacquered and kabuki-backed.

Shearing

Ag Day display
a platform caged
dunk tank of audience eyes

Ewe shouldered in
her lambs before her to distract
They peck to clamp

milk her
punching bag of udders
while she is vised between knees

The shearer says he knows her
anatomy, musculature
where to push harder

when to relent
for the wool to pare in one piece
The shorn bleat from the barn

The lambs release

She kicks up nicked, striated

from where the blades clipped closer

Before the crop is carded

her wool begins to regrow

Karst

Where once ice sheets shucked shale
to round the clints like hips,
farmers drill swallets in turloughs,
rushing that which requires wait.

Time continues to till,
ill-equipped for urgency,
permanent as plastic
or the separation of mothers from calves

migrated to the Burren, some with stars
white as marl, to collect winter's
calcium between bellows hollow
like the throats of spring gentians.

Gnarled grikes funnel rain beneath us
to streams invisible, like ache.
They will stay swallowed, with
or without the tide's heist.

Stars Die Red

In the disquieted cold, stars loop

fusion reactions, build might

by shrinking, collapse

to iron seamed in the striped

hides of Roussillon cliffs mined

for ochre. It's why most barns are red;

not to foreshadow slaughter—

battened steers jostled

down the chute, stripped like chassis,

drained on hooks, portioned to pounds

for carmine-coated mouths that order,

eat: red inside red inside

Broth

The day is soaked and twined like bird's nest soup —
a knockoff of the best (Thai swiftlet)
the high cliffs are scraped to make.

Sometimes I can see them, homeless,
wings folded like a heart on their backs,
stunted by crowd apathy,

biding the basins to sweat out
their runoff, the grasses
to drown in drought.

Hollowed

The maple blushes its leaves to apple skins
then weans them to half-mast. The black
walnut also disbands, litters its apostrophes,
leaving the lawn confused as static.
Its roots finger through the false fronts
of horizons, bootlegging juglone.

Swollen grosgrain cottages, the pumpkins
tamp their circumference estates,
leveling with weight the hay
that forces the rot from inside out—
a visit purpose enough from here on.

No one confesses that the loved ones
are not dead but ossifying in cascades
like the Calibrachoa's trumpets trailing,
desiccated, osteoporotic in window boxes.
Only the weeds are dredged in seed heads.

The rinds have been raked with music wires,
flesh planed into webs that glow the somnambulant flame.
Slovenly solid in deletions, they are left
to their surroundings—trephined,
shank gouged, troweled clean of seeds—
waiting, carved.

Still, Leaf

stark stains on cement,

unleavened

pillories fading to arrows,

corrugated

strands of stems unlaced,

perseverated

In Response

The birds are back, lining the heights—
knit purl knit purl knit purl—stunning
the barren quiet of morning. Why?

There is still snow here—suctioning backwards,
just a bit, for the low branches to poke
through, displayed like public failings—

with more to come. Hell is
the freezing cold. Everything winces,
waters down as the yard and stars go hypothermic.

A bird abandons its hitch, a dropped stitch.
The others stay in their stockinette.
I want to know what it is they know.

The Division

The division is before not between us,

drawn across months like a speed bump,

loitering mostly in spring while we battle

its spine until a second life is awarded.

Hours cycle—spoked scouts promising help

if we lean forth.

To walk backward or recline is to be overrun,

even though the invitation is there.

Mornings, ordinary and indifferent, rummage us.

We maneuver around them

like people in overcrowded hallways

to lay our planks, cross May

and chauffeur the split.

The Awakening of Trust

In this perspective, everything's flat, unlevel;
the bed can't even hold a straight edge.

From here, I can't tell if the sets of shelved
oranges and long-necked vases are pictures

or real. I compare you to the center urn above
the pupil-black door and bet

whether your body would fit if burned to ash.
A sixth of our frame-room was ripped out

then replaced—flatter, grainy like a colored pencil
drawing, bluntly unreflective. Maybe it's time

erasing the tiles, sucking them
one by one into itself. By now I'd say we have 1, 2…

16 years ahead. The floor's eroding, too.
Can we stay forever this way, as you want?

I hope we don't crack the way oil paintings do.
I already feel 300 years old, rubbed away in places.

But you keep to me, minnow-eyed and shooting-star-browed.
It's enough to inflate my seams to snakes that will writhe

stage left if I unloose them, knot in hand. It's my choice
to wear next to nothing now, to become the orange.

I've begun: my soles and fingers drawing
in color like a celery stalk in dyed water. Is this trust

awakening? Parts of me are still crossed, others
crusted with jewels you imprint on me

with the weight of your palm. If gravity reenters,
we will collapse from view like a house of cards.

Given

glass or door cordon,
shrine what began as whim
then reached like nerves
for permanence
through decades that decapitate
and cloud like talc

her body: his yoke

spread where she caught and bloomed,
with a borrowed arm
to illuminate by lamplight—
black and white as blood—
the opening that became a tear

Binary

Pollock "Male and Female, 1942"

You are math,
pure logic, tides of zeros and ones
chalked on igneous rock, on or off.

I am lava, ketchup colored, burning yet burned,
with eyes like paisley fish that will not stop
blinking their gills in breath.

Yours are planetary,
egg moons cycling in the keyhole
of your face. We could lock

but for that x-rayed mass between us—
three perfect diamonds down the center,
an aliquot of you—with edges that measure the stop.

I tend to get lost in that rill where they farm
& farm, quartering and halving myself
in the light motions of begging forgiveness;

wondering, if I fold

myself, could I take shape: an origami swan?

Or would I just be a series of creases,

a stack of pins,

a pile of ones,

on, on, on

while they stay as delicate

as fan coral, corraded if touched. Like them, we

sway—rooted, weighted in rock, see-through

in our dendritic stretching, crossing and weaving always

to live ahead of consolation, orbiting & orbiting.

We are the homesick in our push for the familiar—

never able to leave what was is.

Marriage, Day One

Dance-tired they decided to wait until the honeymoon alarm
parted the light-locking curtains patterned in Matisse
      arabesques.

The picture window premiered vertebrae highways, tangles of
      wires,
platyrrhine bumpers imbricating parking spots.

Life became a shadow box—two cutouts stuck forever in snow,
      photo real,
post fanfare like snuffed candles with rings of sagging
      honeycomb.

His eyes were concentric, flat-glassed as he motioned like a
      typist.
She imagined his face as sample headshots she could pick
      through, then choose.

Cantilevered, her bones attempted to translate in calcium
      apologies—
beached, shunted or crying—that he acts as if he is losing
      someone else.

The drawn bath emptied overnight.
The petals sank in acceptance, love, or something wet.

Homes Are Hell

I.

Dust does not settle, it maroons.
Unable to immix, it encases, uncommitted.
I replaster the cracks of slow collapse,
though the earth heaves, imperceptibly,
then assumes all returns,
whether a trough of walkway
or a building let burn.

Webbed, the snow melts
between the cadence of shingles.
Islands of pigment on the ceiling form,
soft enough to put a finger through.
For those I pretend I am ladderless.

II.

The crash left you crowded;
darning in darkness the clear,
steadfast boundary to the past,
where our bond wisped off

like the rising heat of mirage,

or the contours of a Patterson map—

all inference, no fact.

If beauty remains there,

I will prove it to be

lacelike before it denatures

to a place I cannot push light.

Locked away in the lab

from the chrysalis of your living death,

structure is deliverance,

the scaling of a queer fish.

I synthesize *Dot* and *Delta*

(a permanent point and change)

to emerge as elegant and knitted

as a cyclol.

III.

Puddles are villainous,

their depths deceptive.

I cleaned you up through the crying—

soaked stockings, splattered smock,

no scrapes.

"There you go . . . there you go":
my chant as I smoothed your back,
actually consoling my self subsumed,
unable to be dyed to differentiation
like pearl tapioca or the contents of a cell.

Nobler work could be done
if I was not the constant on call.
The crèche accepts you daily,
ever-willing, patience pure, if paid.
Permanence is at stake;
Pauling's foot on my algorithm's throat,
asphyxiating my trace.

Awoken by your terrors, I furl
around you like a cotyledon,
stroke your hair steeped in sweat,
your arms and legs as if petals.
We are false and in fifths.
There you go.

We Are Not Synesthetes

Yellow can swell like an infected throat, like clots

of forsythia blossoming garish mouths of suasion

that outlast a breath-weight freeze easily.

Pink can burgeon like a double aortic arch, like potted

azaleas root-bound, cawing to be unwound before

blooms fall calmly.

Red can inflame like a rheumatic joint, like spotted

geraniums veining out leaves palmately, petals bloodshot,

raising and expelling seed to colonize benignly.

But our reason is sober, hollow like the fish ribs

pounded for bone meal. Touch is deaf,

playing mountainous when flat as a gurney

through the footworn path to our doss.

Bones of Luray II

Beneath you my bones,

cross-hatched like kindling,

dreamt of nicking

flint to flame to be freed.

Physics played its typecast role,

delivering you intact to me,

a bookmark in a book unread.

You took up like a vagrant

under a trestle; this cavern

our diving bell or a weed

far-reaching, wrong.

Luckily, you dissolved quickly

like salt on the tongue.

Skin is tape, a weak adhesive.

Until discovered we stayed

two transparent maps overlaid.

Cast Waltz

In a room where glass should frame Yara,
past the Picasso harlequin clones
and Bather triangles disjointed,
there are nails placed where our eyes should meet

her body in the brush, open, bare;
the landscape of a lover's fake sea,
with the minted left hand of a wife,
a private twenty years of mourning.

Here you held me, the ground of nowhere,
casting fault lines as taut as parchment
that when quaked or torn told you to take
all illumed, the given, in pieces.

Förlåt Mig

—the only Swedish that stuck after one

semester of Bergman, screenings each Monday,

twice; us newly apart, isolated like close-ups.

Splice. An incision made,

never completely sewn shut.

The stitches climb you like vines,

quick as sleight of hand; their tendrils, though lesser,

belay, reach to crown you—who

in keeping above blame lay blessed.

The mockingbird scouts its perch on the Åkerö

bound to an espalier, wagering whether we will

decode its mimic of sirens and croaks, its song's sham.

We won't.

Constrained like a nest, I feed it my heart—

hoarse yet clutch—invoking its 400 tongues

to translate ceding into song, to graft to you my

one remaining phrase: *forgive me.*

44

Pica

Shamelessly cinematic, the clouds lid
the maladroit light that ebbs through
before-storm leaves scrimmaging
like ants in a disrupted nest.

Shadows draw attention as they are dropped.
Everything as is, no mind to height.
Far-off caws echo in black irises intersected
like saltires; in nightshades, aphid-eaten.

Behind glass you mouth in Morse,
panes looming a cross; your face
a weft warning storm. I want
to eat erosion, pelletize and expel it

as an owl does indigestible bone.
Sediment is safe: cleanly lined
like picket gates, layered and filled like cake.

Jaw Sonnets

I. The End of May

White sheet over blood,
you, gurney-held,
fluorescents above
swell
where I stood:
two lives tried, spearing like Gemini
who hand out hurt, then step aside.

Splayed like a spent bud,
your teeth in foil held
(my hands' strange cud),
their enamel shelled,
less white than surgical gloves.

A respirator times your sighs;
wing doors widen, then collide.

II. Come Alive Confused

I know what you look like dead:
tub-slung head choked on tongue,
arms spread like cherry stems,
eyes pitted with focus flung
past a sea whose waves tear
when a child's screams embark
like tetched animals paired,
floundering toward an ark.

You come alive confused,
sidelong in chagrin, spine slack—
a Grand Odalisque—no, muse
who buoys words out of the black
granite facets inside the sirens
amid spaces, erasing what rends.

Late Collected

The hills hit pause when sleet taps us awake —
its hiss caving in to snow when, late collected,
we hike, gloves like bricks in our hands.

Molted needles, bits of bark fallen like vowels
from a marquee, broomed by wind into ruts
pressed through pleats of trail,
snow augering after them.

We anthropomorphize the sediment in cliff faces —
cardinal, snake or ghost (the one who haunts
your room, where Roosevelt smoked before a hunt) —

while catching breath at the family plot,
birches stark, sloping like the Baldwin's gravestones.
I wind my finger along the first name of the wife,
guessing it is she who haunts you.

Now that it is yours, the stream expects
you to restore its rush each spring when siphoned
into a slighter strand or stopped

with skeins of sticks plowed by ice I watch

break off, slush and run in rugose rafts.

The cistern marks the descent back to the house.

Inside, light or fire disinters your ghosts.

Whether uxorial or Roosevelt, they do not caterwaul

or extend arms like the pine's limbless lintels,

but march and list under unblotted sky,

turning face back to stone.

Treading

The roosters are pecking the shadows
in gravel, crowing over what the sun takes;
their gaits throwing up small tantrums of dust,
hocking their sickles to the grass —
they lie like attenuated oil slicks.

Snowed-in by a room of white
where I don't dare move, a cradle
beneath your head, a bookend heavy
as wet sand, soaked in the drone
of my percussions; your mouth rooting, rooting.

How long will you seek comfort
through the memory of me — our being one
from your beginning, my beginning?

The roosters tread closer on their route
through the columns of condos,
ticking their spurs like clock hands,
twitching their combs, telegraphing: *I forget, I forget.*

What do I do? Count the popcorns

on the ceiling, fall asleep, too? The roosters

dit and dah.

                  It is all aging

as you crow your breaths and shift to slide

away to a body separate.

Night Lane Closures

Truck mud flaps pitch lice of mist
at the windshield—remnants of rain
sloughed by cloud cover, now shelved flatlines,
future movements undisclosed. Brake lights
flick on and off like temporary needs,
distrusting the traction of micro-milled hashes
on the lanes tightly lined by dividers
blistered with reflectors, pushing
us to merge—grains of sand
nested in the neck of an hourglass.

Is aim easier sustained
when slowing or slowed?

The night crew, hazed by fog,
paves the pocks under portable light.
Marrowless ahead, the tunnel ensconces
eventual release from the backhoe of night
that grabbles our vacancies, scripted and steel.

Descent

Stride into stifled sway;
sun striated, sinewed, sloped
like mooring secured
in curves of coral craning
to shelter pelts of silver-flesh
paillettes feeding: sharp
snaps of maracas over
bone-conducted breath
that redress the culling
by wind through waves' work.

Decoys

In this silence is the noisy past
of wishing for silence.
Each cilium tends its frequency
like a fisher his line.

Words are bait

we whet and miter kaleidoscopic
like cut glass or a fly's eye;
their prisms compound shadows
conjured behind translucent scrim
that, if unveiled, would be marked
as starkly as decoys

of Canada geese: heads, necks, beaks
black as Quaker guns (eyes, too,
if they had them); white chinstraps
applied like Band-Aids.

They jut up, C'd and ocular,
among harvested cornstalks

stiff as shorn doll hair,

jagged like snapped toothpicks.

How few it takes to trick;

mirage the coverts, the quills,

life—the danger, I suppose,

of often standing still,

breathing imperceptibly.

Depth collapses in aerial view.

Deer get fooled by black silhouettes

of dogs. Just two

can quell curiosity,

re-route the hunt for sustenance.

Here we are: hooked

or repelled— the brain's lazy design,

the reflex to jigsaw a fit or flee;

this minor litmus of risk

adjourns reason, drives us

like stakes into the dirt of instinct.

Look. Circle. Look again.

Don't land. Our hunters
are camped in stands, camouflaged
by canopies left antlered,
lorn of leaves.

Rest is death divulged,
a capitulation to the fall,
aimless like sleet
or shot geese.

Your Face on the News

Hazy like a snow cloud lengthened low
in the extended light of March,
grist for the grinding: your face on the news,
locked to a truth receded.

In the extended light of March,
letters left blank as winter,
locked to a truth receded—
its cost threadbare; its wear uneven.

Letters left blank as winter,
to reach you before was a loss—
its cost threadbare; its wear uneven.
The mind is an off-center tread.

To reach you before was a loss
carrying its weight with a noose.
The mind is an off-center tread,
which reels itself in on headlines.

Carrying its weight with a noose

thick as the Sunday edition,

which reels itself in on headlines,

your name spelled correctly but mispronounced.

Thick as the Sunday edition,

a drama drawn with a newscaster's story;

your name spelled correctly but mispronounced

in descriptions of gone dogs and what became

a drama drawn with a newscaster's story

(hazy like a snow cloud lengthened low)

in descriptions of gone dogs and what became

grist for the grinding: your face on the news.

The Boredom of Horses

Repetition pares us down to few notable moments
gesturing in traceless flight, moving away endlessly in
redshifts—no roots

foraging in a crawl to strength, browsing with the same
boredom of horses that pinch the grass to stubble, or shrugging
Doric shoulders of Braille to emboss the ground.

Dovetailed with wear, these moments loosen like Zelkova bark.
Love them now because they are lost, because they
hover, posthumous, in memory's quiet corners.

Elephant Funeral

Broken calm of migration.

Bolts of gray phalanx around the matriarch.

She is skeleton-scattered: broken spokes,

joints dissolved in the brush burned earth.

They break.

Egg-and-dart toes tap each bone.

Trunks wind umbilical around ribs

pitted like travertine. They are strummed silently

through the air like a priest tolling his lantern of incense.

Each contour of skull is gripped and released —

a kneading of *without*. They sense that fate is built-in,

that they are joined lastly by gravity, dropped to fossilize.

In sways of wading they retreat

with plaster casts of touch,

trudging to where the sky lets go.

Takes

The script calls for a clown, so they paint you.
Pasted houses and yards arrange, posture
amid the candle, the umbrella, your bruised rehearsals.
You: the ephemeral canary offered up as a prop.

The lines pool in your eyes, wax-hardened;
words pixeled and out of order,
overlaid with a pane of weather,
stars viewed through skylight.

Tendered applause italicizes the mistakes,
snaps them clean till *hey, ho*
sprouts into a static cheer for the disease
fleecing past seconds (shot but not yet dead),

overgrown walkways spanning like spotted carpet.
Each take, longer than finality,
scales your coir beard, somersaults,
then opens to snow.

for Gunnar Björnstrand

Reversal

Let us say good-bye, now,
before you disappear,
in the way I know you,
up the switchback corded
with Quaking Aspens
tremoring shushes
to a wood otherwise petrified,

while I continue on
to the cliff face,
sit down, inch to its edge,
view a valley that remains vast—
at once flat and deep
like the stilted screen
of your face, a Wildt marble,
expressing through angle
of eyelid or tilt of head,
unease with nothing said.

I want you to know it will always be
softness between us, as it has been
from today down through
this umbilical path,
which now must be
retraced by photograph.

Breath Dirge

Up over away like wake you went.

Sanctioned by wayward silence we sit,

lowering eyelids, looking how owls look:

vigilance spent, diurnal motionlessness,

moved by sleep's breath dirge.

This day will be cast in char forever forward.

Any light, a waste. Cold:

our excuse for walls and abandoned wanderings.

We will read to find each other again.

We will sit and listen,

listen,

to accept ourselves as songless.

For a First Poem

Radar is more prescient than rain—
blips and sweeps have us believing
it will come, it will coat, it will cancel.

But you said *magic*. I remember. You
are right: Doppler is discord in this belief.
What will I be?

                Standing uneven, palms
up, remapping lifelines that, once parallel, formed
our bower, though false an aegis as cathedrals.
I need to remember, if the time comes: undam
the tributaries when rain *is* radar; trust

your face, kind-swept, to explain all
I would not know, chipping away
with ancient tools, like Fiorelli pouring
plaster to make casts of the void:

what seemingly comes of nothing was always there,
not waiting among cloud-lost moments in hardened ash,
but latent in every carbon speck of soil,
resurrected only by rain.

Almond, Eyeless

Sometimes, more than I admit, I go
back, a want for haunting that can,
stirred by dream, reverse your fossilization.

Dug up from your protected valley, in rote:
casting feed, unlatching gates, smoking
out the swarms. The air stirs the canopy
to release its stockade, eclipsing shade with petals
of light as we toll in the hammock's netted arc,
where time broadens and will wait—
as if this life aloft, wind-kicked like kites,
can be caught and held without blare
and with you there incant in perfect collocation.

True, this you is ersatz. Yes, it is
myself I actually seek, back
on the better side of becoming,
watertight as a hull.
I am bored: listless and drilled-through.

When awoken from metronomic séance,
all is lost, a hive flown from,
indehiscent as an almond,
eyeless as chain link.

Coda

"A lament in one ear, maybe,
but always a song in the other."

- Sean O'Casey

In seeing what was sought set—
colors creped, burred by mental night—
a coda lofts, then leads
as water leads, downhill—
seeking dissolution in ocean,
a fission of waves that command,
attention and woe.

There you meet me, calm
where I storm, melismatic
as a hymn, which leavens
all that is left in lieu of you.

Bicycle Seconds

When the world has been smoked—elephant gray,
plane-delayed—all there's left to do is play
cards with a pack of Bicycle Seconds, No. 808,

red-backed with riders imaged in discs, bowl cuts and plumage,
handlebars in their grips like jackhammers or the mute,
pursed mouths of the kings, queens, jacks in each suit,

a Siamese twin, no legs, reflected from their patterned waists.
The odds of holding them flush are the same as weather abating
on schedule. So we shuffle, deal the rounds and patiently wait

for the clouds to rub clean of disease in a miracle healing,
and the gulls, like angelless wings, to rise from the field
where the rider steps from his bike and walks out of the wheel.

NOTES

"Anita" makes reference to the hearing of Anita Hill and Senators Howell Heflin, Arlen Specter and Vice President of the United States Joe Biden (a Senator at the time).

"Bones of Luray" and "Bones of Luray II" are fictional accounts of two sets of skeletons found intermingled, though dated to separate, unrelated accidents, in Luray Caverns, Luray, Virginia.

"Coda" borrows the term *mental night* from sculptor Adolfo Wildt.

"Ebb" refers to Ebb Cade, later named HP-12 (Human Product-12), a construction worker at Clinton Engineer Works in Oak Ridge, TN. Girls of Atomic City is borrowed from the title, *The Girls of Atomic City: The Untold Story Of The Women Who Helped Win World War II*, by Denise Kiernan.

"Given" takes its title from part of the work by Marcel Duchamp, *Étant donnés: 1. La chute d'eau, 2. Le gaz d'éclairage.*

"Hadley" refers to Hadley Richardson.

"Homes are Hell" takes its title from an essay by Dorothy (Dot, Delta) Wrinch, who inspired the viewpoint of the poem regarding herself, her husband and her daughter. Warren Weaver once described Wrinch as a "queer fish".

"Kate at Rader" refers to The Rader Institute.

"Late Collected" refers to Baldwin Cemetery, West Dover, VT.

"For a First Poem" was written in response to my son's first poem at age 6, reproduced below, with permission.

Mud Hut

There's a place that nobody knows,

That when it rains,

It builds itself magically.

It is something that is brown —

That you would not know.

And it is my home.

Reference is also made to Giuseppe Fiorelli.

"The Awakening of Trust" takes its title from the detail of a page from the *Rasamanjari* of Bhanudatta series ascribed to Devadasa, dated 1694-95. The Alvin O. Bellak Collection.

Acknowledgements

Grateful acknowledgement is made to the editors of the following publications, in which some of these poems first appeared, sometimes in slightly different form:

Blackbird: "Treading"

The Hollins Critic: "Bicycle Seconds"

Subtropics: "Charged with Error", "Decoys", "Karst", "Shearing", "Stars Die Red", "Still, Leaf"

Thank you to

My husband, for being my first and best reader, if I was to be understood by anyone, I am glad it was you

My son, for instilling the courage to let these poems live outside myself

My family, for their solidarity and acceptance

James Tate Hill and Daniel Coudriet, for their encouragement and examples of tenacity

Nancy Rosenberger and Larry MacKenzie, for sharing their Light

Tessa Cheek, for being a fellow eagle eye

RHWD, for seeing something in someone who sees this, I will carry your kindness, generosity, and humor with me, always

This book was designed and set in Palatino Linotype by RHWD Industries

Cover art by Francesca Myman

Photograph of the author by Jennifer Monson

Printed by Salem Printing

groundhog
POETRY PRESS